FAC-SIMILES

OF THE

MEMORIAL STONES

OF THE

LAST ENGLISH ANCESTORS

OF

GEORGE WASHINGTON

IN THE PARISH CHURCH OF BRINGTON, NORTHAMPTONSHIRE, ENGLAND;

PERMANENTLY PLACED IN THE

State House of Massachusetts.

BOSTON:

WILLIAM WHITE, PRINTER TO THE STATE.

1862.

Commonwealth of Massachusetts.

EXECUTIVE DEPARTMENT, COUNCIL CHAMBER,
BOSTON, March 15, 1861.

To the Honorable the House of Representatives :

I have the honor to present to the General Court, as a gift to the Commonwealth of Massachusetts from one of its citizens, certain memorials of great historic interest.

The home and final resting-place of the ancestors of GEORGE WASHINGTON were until recently unvisited by, and unknown to, Americans. In the genealogical table, appended to the "Life of Washington" by our distinguished fellow-citizen, Mr. Jared Sparks, it is stated that Lawrence Washington, the father of John Washington (who emigrated to Virginia in 1657), was buried at Brington ; but though both Mr. Sparks and Washington Irving visited Sulgrave, an earlier home of the Washingtons, neither of these learned biographers appears by his works to have repaired to this quiet parish in Northamptonshire.

Our fellow-citizen, the Hon. Charles Sumner, on a recent visit to England, identified certain inscriptions in the parish-church of Brington, near Althorp, as being those of the father and uncle of John Washington, the emigrant to Virginia, who was the great-grandfather of the Father of his Country.

Earl Spencer, the proprietor of Althorp, so honorably known as an early advocate of Parliamentary reform, sought out the quarry from which, more than two centuries ago, these tablets were taken, and caused others to be made which are exact *fac-similes* of the originals. These he has presented to

Mr. Sumner, who has expressed the desire that memorials, so interesting to all Americans, may be placed where they may be seen by the public, and has authorized me to offer them to the Commonwealth, if it be the pleasure of the legislature to order them to be preserved in some public part of the State House.

I send with this a letter addressed to myself by the learned historian of Washington, bearing testimony to the great interest of these memorials, and expressing the desire that they may (Mr. Sumner assenting) be placed in the capitol.

A letter from Mr. Sumner to Mr. Sparks also accompanies this Message, describing the church at Brington, and some of the associations which cluster around the resting-place of the ancestors of our Washington.

JOHN A. ANDREW.

MR. SPARKS TO THE GOVERNOR.

CAMBRIDGE, 22d February, 1861.

DEAR SIR:—I enclose a copy of a highly interesting letter from Mr. Charles Sumner, describing the church at Brington, near Althorp, in Northamptonshire. In this church were deposited the remains of Lawrence Washington, who was the father of John and Lawrence Washington, the emigrants to America, and who was therefore the last English ancestor of George Washington. A copy of the inscription on the stone which covers the grave of Lawrence Washington, and also of another inscription over the grave of his brother Robert Washington, who was buried in the same church, are given with exactness in Mr. Sumner's letter. As far as I am aware, these inscriptions are now for the first time made known in this country.

Earl Spencer has sent to Mr. Sumner two stones, being from the same quarry, and having the same form and dimensions, as the originals, and containing a *fac-simile* of the inscriptions. It has been suggested that these stones ought to be placed in the State House, where they may be accessible to the public, and my opinion on the subject has been asked. As they are unquestionably genuine memorials of the Washington family, and possess on this account a singular historical interest, I cannot imagine that a more appropriate disposition of them could be made. I understand that Mr. Sumner would cheerfully assent to such an arrangement, and I cannot doubt that your Excellency will be well inclined to take such measures as may effectually aid in attaining so desirable an object.

I am, Sir, very respectfully yours,

JARED SPARKS.

His Excellency JOHN A. ANDREW,
Governor of Massachusetts.

MR. SUMNER TO MR. SPARKS.

BOSTON, 22d November, 1860.

MY DEAR SIR: — Since our last conversation Earl Spencer has kindly sent to me precise copies of the two "Memorial Stones" of the English family of George Washington, which I have already described to you as harmonizing exactly with the pedigree which has the sanction of your authority. These are of the same stone, and of the same size, with the originals, and have the original inscriptions, — being in all respects *fac-similes.* They will, therefore, give you an exact idea of those most interesting memorials in the parish-church of Brington, near Althorp, in Northamptonshire.

The largest is of Lawrence Washington, the father of John Washington, who emigrated to America. It is a slab of bluish-gray sandstone, and measures five feet and nine inches long and two feet and six inches broad. Here is the inscription: —

HERE·LIETH·THE·BODI·OF·LAVRENCE
WASHINGTON·SONNE·&·HEIRE·OF
ROBERT·WASHINGTON·OF·SOVLGRAE
IN·THE·COVNTIE·OF·NORTHAMTON
ESQVIER·WHO·MARIED·MARGARET
THE·ELDEST·DAVGHTER·OF·WILLIAM
BVTLER·OF·TEES·IN·THE·COVNTIE
OF·SVSSEXE·ESQVIER·WHO·HAD·ISSV
BY·HER·8·SONNS·&·9·DAVGHTERS
WHICH·LAVRENCE·DECESSED·THE·13
OF·DECEMBER·A: DÑI: 1616

THOV·THAT·BY·CHANCE·OR·CHOYCE
OF·THIS·HAST·SIGHT
KNOW·LIFE·TO·DEATH·RESIGNES
AS·DAYE·TO·NIGHT
BVT·AS·THE·SVNNS·RETORNE
REVIVES·THE·DAYE
SO·CHRIST·SHALL·VS
THOVGH·TVRNDE·TO·DVST·&·CLAY

Above the inscription, carved in the stone, are the arms of the Washingtons, with the arms of the Butlers *impaled*, the latter being, in the language of heraldry, *azure, a chevron between three covered cups or*.

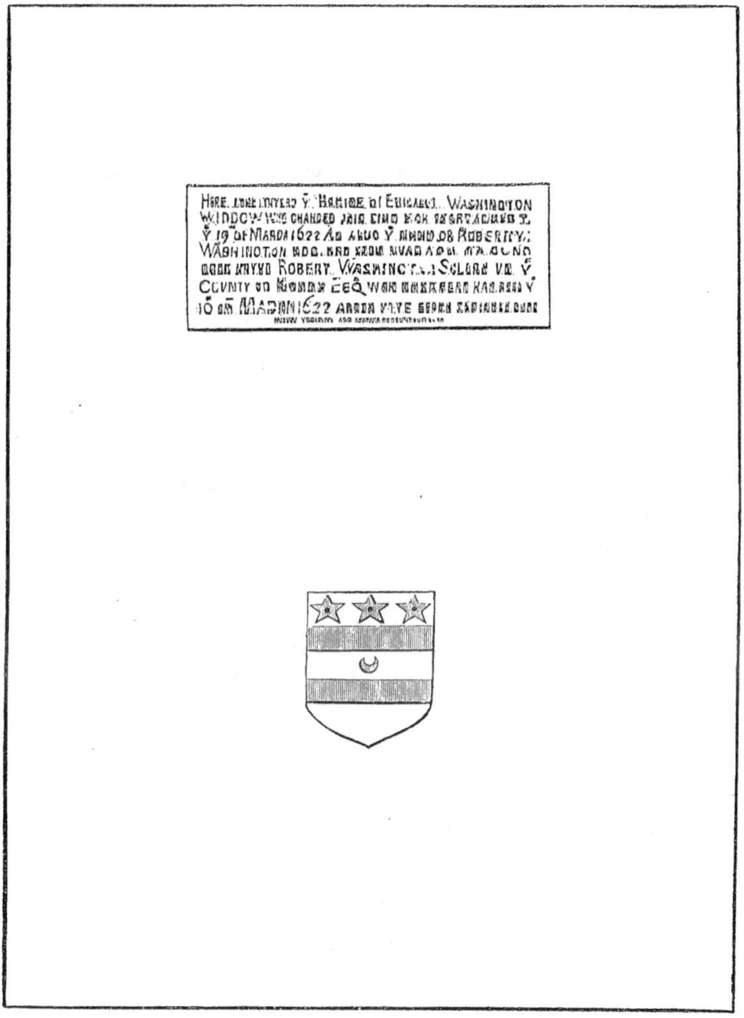

The other stone is placed over Robert Washington and Elizabeth his wife. Robert was the uncle of the emigrant. This is a slab of the same sandstone, and measures three feet and six inches long and two feet and six inches broad. The inscription is on a small brass plate set into the stone, and is as follows:

HERE LIES INTERRED Y^E BODIES OF ELIZAB: WASHINGTON
WIDDOWE, WHO CHANGED THIS LIFE FOR IMORTALLITIE
Y^E 19TH OF MARCH 1622· AS ALSO Y^E BODY OF ROBERT
WASHINGTON GENT: HER LATE HVSBAND SECOND
SONNE OF ROBERT WASHINGTON OF SOLGRAVE IN Y^E
COVNTY OF NORTH: ESQ^R: WHO DEPTED THIS LIFE Y^E
10TH OF MARCH 1622· AFTER THEY LIVED LOVINGLY TOGETHER
MANY YEARES IN THIS PARRISH

On a separate brass, beneath the inscription, are the arms of the Washingtons without any addition but a crescent, the *mark of cadency* that denotes the *second* son. These, as you are well aware, have the combination of stars and stripes, and are sometimes supposed to have suggested our national flag. In heraldic language, they are *argent, two bars gules, in chief three mullets* (or *stars*) *of the second.*

In the interesting chapter on the "Origin and Genealogy of the Washington Family," which you give in the Appendix to your "Life of Washington," it appears that Lawrence, the father of the emigrant, died 13th December, and was buried at Brington 15th December, 1616. But the genealogical tables, which you followed, gave no indication of the locality of this church. Had it appeared that it was the parish-church of the Spencer family, in Northamptonshire, the locality, which I believe has not been heretofore known in our country, would have been precisely fixed.

In point of fact, the slab which covers Lawrence Washington is in the chancel of the church, by the side of the monuments of the Spencer family. These are all in admirable preservation, with full-length effigies, busts, or other sculptural work, and exhibit an interesting and connected series of sepulchral memorials, from the reign of Henry the Eighth to the present time. Among them is a monument by the early English sculptor, Nicholas Stone; another by Nollekens from a design by Cipriani; and another by Flaxman, with exquisitely beautiful personifications of Faith and Charity. Beneath repose the successive representatives of this illustrious family, which has added to its aristocratic claims by services to the State, and also by the unique and world-famous library collected by one of its members. In this companionship will be found the last English ancestor of our Washington.

The other slab, covering Robert, the uncle of the emigrant, is in one of the aisles, where it is scraped by the feet of all who pass.

The parish of Brington (in modern pronunciation *Brighton*) is between seven and eight miles from the town of Northampton, not far from the centre of England. It is written in Domesday Book "Brinintone" and also "Brintone." It contains about 2,210 acres, of which about 1,490 acres belong to Earl Spencer, about 326 acres to the rector in right of his church, and about 130 acres to other persons. The soil is in general a dark-colored loam with a small tract of clay towards the north. Nearly four-fifths of the whole is pasture and feeding land.

In the village still stands the house said to have been occupied by the Washingtons when the emigrant brother left them. You will see a vignette of it on the title-page of the recent English work, entitled *The Washingtons.* Over the door are carved the words, THE LORD GEVETH, THE LORD TAKETH AWAY, BLESSED BE THE NAME OF THE LORD; while the Parish Register gives a pathetic commentary by showing, that, in the very year when this house was built, a child had been born and another had died in this family.

The church, originally dedicated to the Virgin, stands at the north-east angle of the village, and consists of an embattled tower with five bells, a nave, north and south aisles, a chancel, a chapel, and a modern porch. The tower is flanked by buttresses of two stages. The present fabric goes back in its origin to the beginning of the fourteenth century, nearly two hundred years before the discovery of America. The chancel and chapel, where repose the Spencers and Lawrence Washington, were rebuilt by Sir John Spencer, the purchaser of the estate, at the beginning of the sixteenth century. They afford one of the latest specimens of the Tudor style of architecture. The church is beautifully "situated on the summit of the highest ground of Brington," and is surrounded by a stone wall, lined with trees. Dibdin says, that a more complete picture of a country churchyard is rarely seen. A well-trimmed walk encircles the whole of the interior, while the fine Gothic windows at the end of the chancel fill the scene with picturesque beauty.

The Register of the Parish, which is still preserved, commences in 1560. From this it appears that William Proctor was the rector from 1601 to 1627, covering the period of the last of the Washingtons there. The following further entries occur, relating to this family:

1616. "Mr. Lawrance Washington was buried the XVth day of December."
1620. "Mr. Philip Curtis and Mis Amy Washington were maried August 8."
1622. "Mr. Robert Washington was buried March ye 11th."
——. "M^rs^. Elisabeth Washington widow was buried March ye 20th."

Of one of the ministers in this church we have an interesting glimpse in Evelyn's Memoirs (Vol. I., p. 652), where the following entry will be found under date of August 18th, 1688: "Dr. Jeffryes [a misnomer for *Jessop*], the minister of Althorp, who was my Lord's chaplain when Ambassador in France, *preached the shortest discourse I ever heard;* but what was defective in the amplitude of his sermon, he had supplied in the largeness and convenience of the parsonage-house."

At a short distance — less than a mile — is Althorp, the seat of the Spencers, surrounded by a park of five hundred acres, of which one of the gates opens near the church. There are oak trees, bordering on the church-yard, which were growing at the time of the purchase of the estate in the reign of Henry the Seventh. Evelyn was often here a delighted visitor. On one occasion he speaks of " the house, or rather palace, at Althorp." (Vol. I., p. 652.) In another place he describes it as "placed in a pretty open bottom, very finely watered, and flanked with stately woods and groves in a park." (Vol. I., p. 478.) Let me add, that there is an engraving of Althorp at this time, by the younger Luke Vorsterman, a Dutch artist.

There is one feature of the park which excited the admiration of Evelyn, and at a later day of Mrs. Jameson, who gives to it some beautiful pages in her " Visits and Sketches at Home and Abroad." It is the record of the times when different plantations of trees were begun. While recommending this practice in his " Sylva," Evelyn remarks, " The only instance I know of the like in our country is in the park of Althorp." There are six of these commemorative stones. The first records a wood planted by Sir John Spencer, in 1567 and 1568; the second, a wood planted by Sir John Spencer, son of the former, in 1589; the third, a wood planted by Robert Lord Spencer, in 1602 and 1603; the fourth, a wood planted by Sir William Spencer, Knight of the Bath, afterwards Lord Spencer, in 1624. This stone is ornamented with the arms of the Spencers, and on the back is inscribed, VP AND BEE DOING AND GOD WILL PROSPER. It was in this scenery, and amidst these associations, that the Washingtons lived. When the emigrant left in 1657, these woods must have been well-grown. It was not long afterwards that they arrested the attention of Evelyn.

The Household Books at Althorp show, that for many years the Washingtons were frequent guests there. The hospitality of this seat has been renowned. The Queen of James the First and Prince Henry, on their way to London in 1603, were welcomed there in an entertainment, memorable for a Masque from the vigorous muse of Ben Jonson. (Ben Jonson's Works, Vol. VI., p. 475.) Charles the First was at Althorp in 1647, when he received the first intelligence of the approach of those pursuers from whom he never escaped until his life had been laid down upon the scaffold. In 1695, King William was there for a week, and, according to Evelyn, was "mightily entertained." (Vol. II., p. 30.) At least one of the members of this family was famous for hospitality of a different character. Evelyn records that he used to dine with the Countess of Sunderland,—the title then borne by the Spencers,—"when she invited *fire-eaters*, stone-eaters, and opera-singers, after the fashion of the day." (Vol. I., pp. 458, 483, 579.)

The family was early and constantly associated with literature; Spencer, the poet, belonged to it, and to one of its members he has dedicated his "Tears of the Muses." It was for the same Alice Spencer that Milton is said to have written his "Arcades," and Sir John Harrington has celebrated her memory by an epigram. The Sacharissa of Waller was the Lady Dorothy Sidney, wife of the first Earl of Sunderland, the third Lord Spencer, who perished fighting for King Charles the First at Newbury. I do not dwell on other associations of a later day, as my object is simply to allude to those which existed in the time of the Washingtons.

"The nobility of the Spencers has been illustrated and enriched by the trophies of Marlborough; but I exhort them to consider the Fairy Queen as the most precious jewel of their coronet." Thus wrote Gibbon in his Memoirs, and all must feel the beauty of the passage. Perhaps it is not too much to say, that this nobility may claim another illustration from its ties of friendship and neighborhood with the family of Washington. I cannot doubt that hereafter the parish-church of Brington will be often visited by our countrymen, who will look with reverence upon a spot so closely associated with American history.

I trust that this little sketch, suggested by what I saw at Althorp during a brief visit last autumn, will not seem irrelevant. Besides my own personal impressions and the volumes quoted, I have relied upon Dibdin's "Ædes Althorpianæ," so interesting to all bibliographical students, and especially upon Baker's "History of Northamptonshire," — one of those magnificent local works which illustrate English history — to which you refer in your Appendix.

Of course, the Memorial Stones, which I have received from Lord Spencer, are of much historic value; and I think that I shall best carry out the generous idea of the giver by taking care that they are permanently placed where they can be seen by the public; perhaps in the State House near Chantrey's beautiful statue of Washington, — if this should be agreeable to the Commonwealth.

Pray pardon this long letter, and believe me, my dear Sir, with much regard,

Ever sincerely yours,

CHARLES SUMNER.

JARED SPARKS, Esq.

Commonwealth of Massachusetts.

House of Representatives, March 23, 1861.

The Committee on the State House, to whom was referred the Message of His Excellency the Governor, presenting to the General Court, as a gift from the Hon. Charles Sumner, certain memorials of Washington, of great historic interest, report that they consider it a matter of special congratulation that the interesting facts concerning the Father of his Country, contained in the papers accompanying the Message, should have been first made known to us by a citizen of Massachusetts; and, deeming it important that these valuable memorials should be permanently preserved in the capitol of the State, they report the accompanying resolves.

Per order,

R. WARD.

Resolves in relation to certain Memorials of the Ancestors of Washington.

Resolved, That the thanks of the General Court be and hereby are presented to the Hon. Charles Sumner for his interesting and patriotic gift to the Commonwealth, of two Memorial Tablets in imitation of the originals which mark the final resting-place of the last English ancestors of George Washington.

Resolved, That the Commissioners on the State House cause the same to be prepared and placed, with appropriate inscriptions, in some convenient place in the Doric Hall of the State House, near the Statue of Washington.—*Approved April* 6, 1861.

OFFICE OF THE COMMISSIONERS ON THE STATE HOUSE,
BOSTON, January 1, 1862.

The undersigned, Commissioners on the State House, hereby certify, that, in compliance with the Resolve of the Legislature of Massachusetts, passed April 6, 1861, they have caused the above-named Memorial Tablets of the Washington Family to be permanently placed upon the marble floor of the area in which the Statue of Washington stands, within the railing in front of said Statue.

JOHN MORISSEY, *Sergeant-at-Arms.*
OLIVER WARNER, *Secretary.*
HENRY K. OLIVER, *Treasurer.*

A white marble tablet, placed by the Commissioners near the Washington Memorials, bears the following inscription:

THESE FAC-SIMILES OF THE MEMORIAL STONES OF THE WASHINGTON FAMILY IN THE PARISH CHURCH OF BRINGTON, THE BURIAL-PLACE OF THE SPENCERS NEAR ALTHORP, NORTHAMPTONSHIRE, ENGLAND, WERE PRESENTED BY THE RIGHT HONORABLE EARL SPENCER TO CHARLES SUMNER OF MASSACHUSETTS, AND BY HIM OFFERED TO THE COMMONWEALTH 22 FEBRUARY, 1861.

LAWRENCE WAS FATHER, AND ROBERT UNCLE, OF THE ENGLISH EMIGRANT TO VIRGINIA, WHO WAS GREAT-GRANDFATHER OF GEORGE WASHINGTON.

www.ingramcontent.com/pod-product-compliance
Lightning Source LLC
LaVergne TN
LVHW020639110826
845149LV00004B/1288